AF270680

Taiwan Lantern Festival

by Grace Hansen

WORLD FESTIVALS

Abdo Kids Jumbo is an Imprint of Abdo Kids
abdobooks.com

abdobooks.com

Published by Abdo Kids, a division of ABDO, P.O. Box 398166, Minneapolis, Minnesota 55439.
Copyright © 2023 by Abdo Consulting Group, Inc. International copyrights reserved in all countries.
No part of this book may be reproduced in any form without written permission from the publisher.
Abdo Kids Jumbo™ is a trademark and logo of Abdo Kids.

Printed in the United States of America, North Mankato, Minnesota.

102022

012023

THIS BOOK CONTAINS
RECYCLED MATERIALS

Photo Credits: AP Images, Getty Images, Shutterstock, ©unknown p.7/ CC BY-SA 4.0
Production Contributors: Teddy Borth, Jennie Forsberg, Grace Hansen
Design Contributors: Candice Keimig, Pakou Moua

Library of Congress Control Number: 2021950627
Publisher's Cataloging-in-Publication Data

Names: Hansen, Grace, author.

Title: Taiwan lantern festival / by Grace Hansen.

Description: Minneapolis, Minnesota : Abdo Kids, 2023 | Series: World festivals | Includes online resources
    and index.

Identifiers: ISBN 9781098261795 (lib. bdg.) | ISBN 9781098262631 (ebook) | ISBN 9781098263058
    (Read-to-Me ebook)

Subjects: LCSH: Taiwan--History--Juvenile literature. | Festivals--Taiwan--Juvenile literature. | Manners
    and customs--Juvenile literature. | Festivals--Juvenile literature.

Classification: DDC 394.2683--dc23

Table of Contents

Taiwan Lantern Festival

The Taiwan Lantern Festival takes place on the first full moon of the new lunar year. The lunar calendar is very important in Taiwan and to Buddhists. People celebrate the special day with many traditions.

Asia
China
South
Korea
Japan
Taiwan
Philippines
Pacific
Ocean
N
S
E
W

5

Lantern Festival Origins

Lantern festivals date back more than 2,000 years. These celebrations are often linked to Emperor Mingdi of the Han **dynasty**. During his rule, **Buddhism** began to spread into China.

白馬寺
Emperor Mingdi

It is told that the emperor saw
Buddhist monks light **temple**
lanterns. The monks always did
this on the fifteenth day of the
first lunar month. The emperor
wanted everyone else to do
the same.

中央毘盧遮那佛

China has celebrated the Lantern Festival for centuries. Taiwan is an island nation off the coast of China. It has held its own Lantern Festival since 1990.

The Taiwan Lantern Festival Today

Traditionally, celebrators carry hand lanterns. But it is normal to see larger and more exciting lanterns throughout Taiwan. They can be all shapes and sizes!

People often write wishes on their lanterns. Some believe that when they release their lantern, they are letting go of their past self. They look forward to good luck in the new year.

Each year, the festival **debuts** a

main lantern. It is more than 30

feet (9 m) tall! It lights up while

beautiful music plays.

One of the most popular foods at the festival is a type of **dumpling**. It is prepared using sweet and solid fillings. Then it is rolled in rice flour. It looks like a full moon.

Happy Lantern Festival
鬧元宵
19

A huge celebration then takes place in Yanshui. It is called the Yanshui Beehive Fireworks Festival. Hundreds of thousands of firecrackers go off at once. It looks like bees flying from their hives!

The Main Festival Lantern and the Chinese Zodiac

The main lantern at the Taiwan Lantern Festival often reflects the animal symbol of the year in the Chinese zodiac. Find the year you were born below. Do you share similar traits with that animal?

Rat
1996, 2008, 2020
- savvy
- cunning
- successful

Ox
1997, 2009, 2021
- strong
- stable
- persistent

Tiger
1998, 2010, 2022
- lively
- cheerful
- independent

Rabbit
1999, 2011, 2023
- sensitive
- creative
- friendly

Dragon
2000, 2012, 2024
- passionate
- strong
- determined

Snake
2001, 2013, 2025
- wise
- brave
- intuitive

Horse
2002, 2014, 2026
- optimistic
- cheerful
- successful

Goat
2003, 2015, 2027
- gentle
- stable
- kind

Monkey
2004, 2016, 2028
- clever
- energetic
- happy

Rooster
2005, 2017, 2029
- punctual
- hard working
- confident

Dog
2006, 2018, 2030
- loyal
- sincere
- kind

Pig
2007, 2019, 2031
- truthful
- reliable
- giving

Glossary

Buddhism – a religion from Asia, founded in the 6th century BCE by Buddha. Buddhism teaches freedom from the self and from one's wants. A Buddhist is someone who follows the teachings of Buddha.

debut – to appear in public for the first time.

dumpling – foods consisting of a flattened piece of dough wrapped around a filling such as meat, vegetables, or fruit and steamed, fried, boiled, or baked.

dynasty – a series of rulers from the same family or group.

temple – a building or place where a god or gods are worshiped.

Index

Abdo Kids
ONLINE
FREE! ONLINE MULTIMEDIA RESOURCES

Visit **abdokids.com** to access crafts, games, videos, and more!

Use Abdo Kids code **WTK1795** or scan this QR code!